ROW, ROW, ROW

Each of these children has something in common with the two others in the same row of pictures. You can see that all three children in the top row across are wearing blue shirts. Look at the other rows across, down, and diagonally. Can you tell what's alike in each row?

Illustrated by John Nez

Answer on page 33.

LOST AND FOUND

It's been a very busy day at the Lost-and-Found Desk. Can you help the clerk return the lost items to their owners? Which item will be left on the shelf?

Answer on page 33.

Oh K!

How many things in this picture begin with the letter K?

Answer on page 33.

HIDDEN PLANETS

The names of all nine planets are hidden in the letters below. Can you find them? Look up, down, sideways, and diagonally. Be careful—some words overlap, and some are written backwards.

```
L M V E N U S O
R O E E A R T H
E S M R K A F P
T A O A C N L R
I T A P R U U R
P U P L T S R E
U R M O O O N Y
J N E P T U N E
```

Illustrated by Barbara Gray

WALKING WIGGLY

Mark is taking his new pet, Wiggly, for a walk. What do you think it is? Use your imagination, and finish this picture.

Illustrated by Holly Kowitt

HOW MANY __ IN A __?

There are 60 s. in a m. That's a quick way to say 60 seconds in a minute. Now that you know the quick system, try these:

1. 3 f. in a y.

2. 7 d. in a w.

3. 4 q. in a g.

4. 12 m. in a y.

5. 12 i. in a f.

6. 2 c. in a p.

7. 60 m. in an h.

8. 365 d. in a y.

9. 24 h. in a d.

10. 52 w. in a y.

Illustrated by Jennifer Skopp

Answer on page 33.

CALL TO ORDER

These pictures are out of order. Can you number them so they tell a story from beginning to end?

Illustrated by John Nez

Answer on page 34.

PICTURE CROSSWORD

These pictures tell you what words to write in the
spaces across ➡ and down ↓ .

SEE WHAT SUE SAW

Sue uses her binoculars wherever she goes. Can you tell where she went each day?

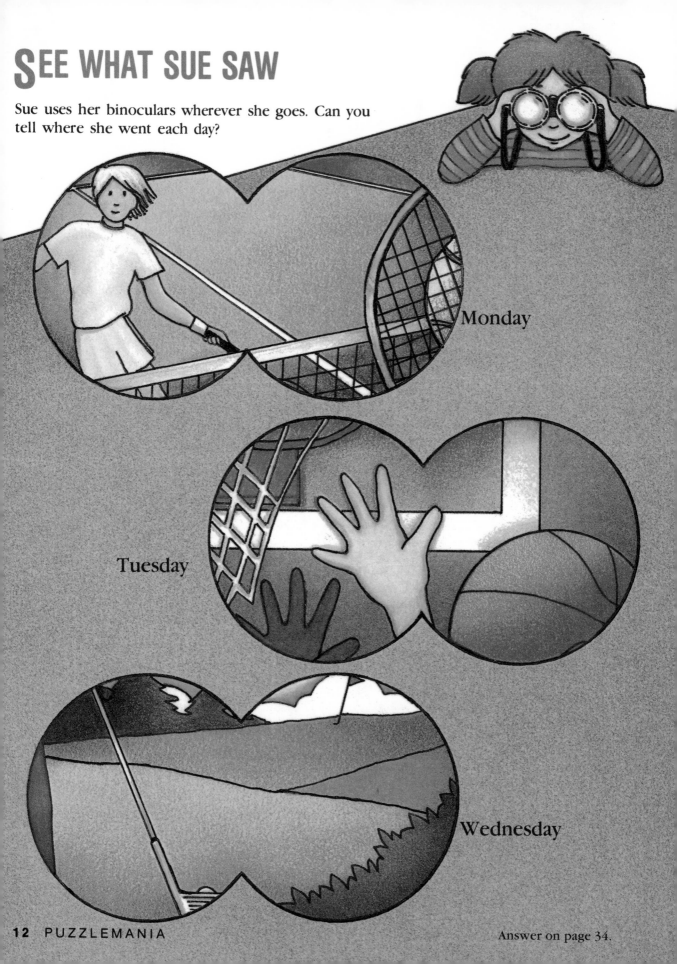

Monday

Tuesday

Wednesday

Answer on page 34.

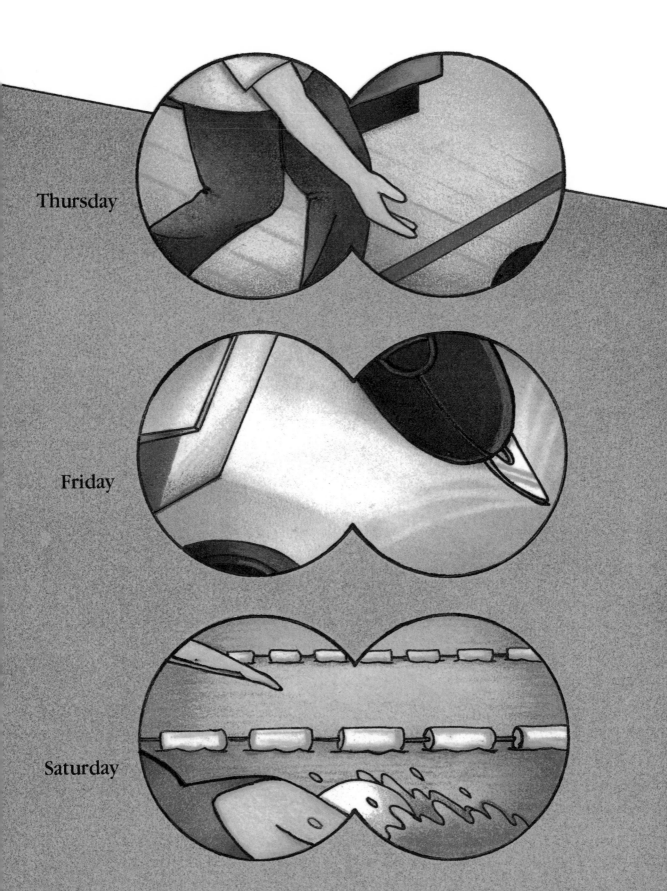

Thursday

Friday

Saturday

MIX-UP AT THE CANDY COMPANY

1.

There's been a mix-up at Alexandra's Candy Company. The barrels are numbered, but no one knows what's in them. The letters on the labels have been scrambled. The one labeled MARASCLE is actually full of CARAMELS. Help Alexandra unscramble the other candy names so she can get back to pulling taffy.

2.

3.

4.

5.

6.

7.

8.

9.

10.

Answer on page 34.

Illustrated by Jerry Zimmerman

HOP TO IT!

Harvey is hurrying home to his hutch. He needs to pick up groceries along the way. There are lots to choose from, but his family eats only raw vegetables. Which way should Harvey go to find foods that rabbits might like?

START

FINISH

Illustrated by Barbara Gray

Answer on page 34.

ALPHABEADS

Start at the top with A. Move up, down, left, right, or diagonally to the nearest B. From there, move to the nearest C. Connect the beads to make an alphabet necklace from A to Z.

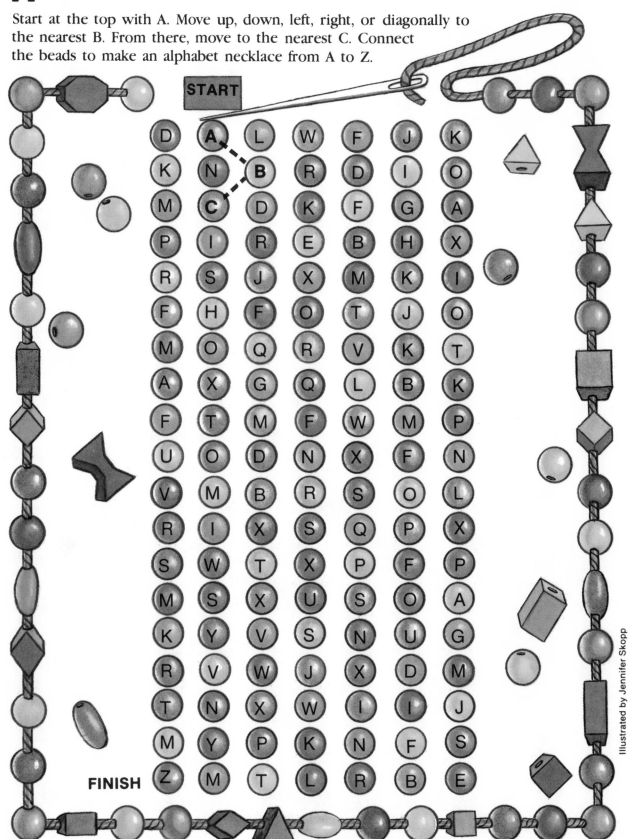

Illustrated by Jennifer Skopp

Answer on page 34.

JUNGLE MEMORIES
Part 1

Take a long look at this picture. Try to remember everything you see in it. Then turn the page and try to answer some questions about it without looking back.

DON'T READ THIS UNTIL YOU HAVE LOOKED AT "Jungle Memories-Part 1" ON PAGE 17

JUNGLE MEMORIES
Part 2

Can you answer these questions about the jungle scene you saw?

1. How many elephants did you see?
2. Was the turtle swimming?
3. Were all the animals right side up?
4. Did the cat have stripes or spots?
5. How many birds were on the vine?

6. Was the man holding an ice-cream cone or a cookie?
7. Which animal held a flower?
8. How many birds were flying?

Answer on page 34.

AT THE FINISH LINE

Pat, Emily, and Amy entered a Soap Box Derby. Each one took a prize. By reading the clues below, can you tell who took first, second, and third place? What color car did each one drive?

Pat beat only the blue car.

The yellow car was not first.

Amy was not driving the red car.

Illustrated by Marc Nadel

Answer on page 34.

WHAT HAVE WE HERE?

Where have you seen these shapes?
How many can you name?

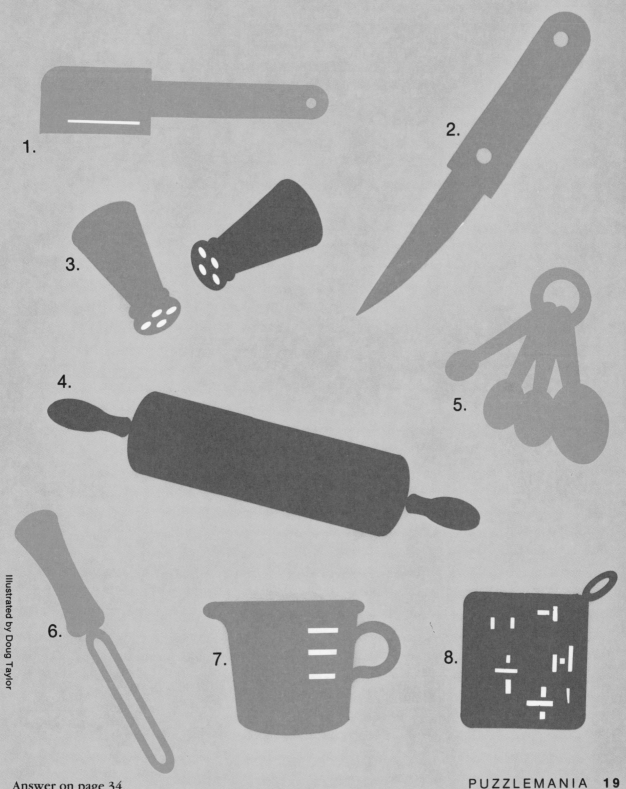

1.

2.

3.

4.

5.

6.

7.

8.

Illustrated by Doug Taylor

Answer on page 34.

TREASURE HUNT

Captain Richman keeps his treasure on a secret island. Starting at the ship, follow the directions on the map from island to island. When you find a letter, stash it away in the ship's locker. Once you reach Richman's Island, the letters will tell you what the captain keeps there.

Illustrated by Terry Kovalcik

SOMETHING FISHY

There are at least ten differences in these two pictures. How many can you find?

WHAT A WAY TO GO!

These explorers are traveling across the country. To find out how they'll get there, connect the red dots from 1 to 31. Then connect the blue dots from A to Z. Bon voyage!

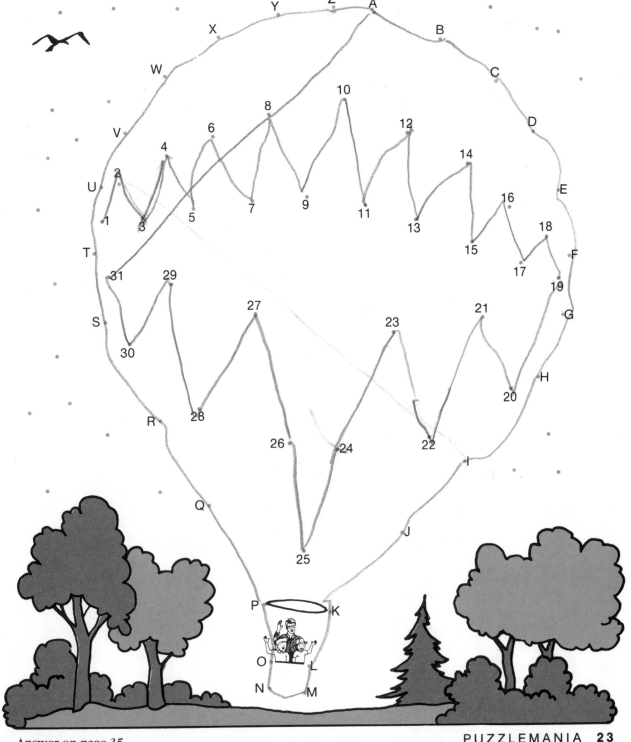

Answer on page 35.

CROSSING THE STATES

The names of all fifty states fit into the spaces on the following page. The lists tell how many letters are in each state name. This will help you see where they fit into the puzzle. Some of the states have been filled in. It may help you to cross each state off the list when you put it in the puzzle.

4 LETTERS
Utah
Ohio
Iowa

5 LETTERS
Maine
Idaho
Texas

6 LETTERS
Nevada
Oregon
Alaska
Kansas
Hawaii

7 LETTERS
Montana
Arizona
Alabama
Indiana
Vermont
New York
Florida
Georgia
Wyoming

8 LETTERS
Oklahoma
Maryland
Colorado
Nebraska
Missouri
Illinois
Michigan
Virginia
Delaware
Kentucky
Arkansas

9 LETTERS
New Mexico
Louisiana
Wisconsin
Tennessee
Minnesota
New Jersey

10 LETTERS
California
Washington

11 LETTERS
South Dakota
North Dakota
Mississippi
Rhode Island
Connecticut

12 LETTERS
New Hampshire
Pennsylvania
West Virginia

13 LETTERS
North Carolina
South Carolina
Massachusetts

UNITED STATES OF AMERICA

GULF OF MEXICO

ILLINOIS

PENNSYLVANIA

NORTHDAKOTA

SOUTHCAROLINA

MONTANA

ALASKA

Answer on page 35.

SQUARE HUNT

Inside this big square are many smaller squares.
How many can you find altogether?

Answer on page 35.

Illustrated by Pat Merr

THE SECRET LISTS

Webster and Wagnall both wanted the job of List Keeper to Queen Elistabeth. They each made a sample list. To keep their lists secret from one another, they each made up a code. Can you tell what's on each list and who wrote it?

This is Webster's code:

A = N	**J** = W	**S** = F
B = O	**K** = X	**T** = G
C = P	**L** = Y	**U** = H
D = Q	**M** = Z	**V** = I
E = R	**N** = A	**W** = J
F = S	**O** = B	**X** = K
G = T	**P** = C	**Y** = L
H = U	**Q** = D	**Z** = M
I = V	**R** = E	

This is Wagnall's code:

A = Z	**J** = Q	**S** = H
B = Y	**K** = P	**T** = G
C = X	**L** = O	**U** = F
D = W	**M** = N	**V** = E
E = V	**N** = M	**W** = D
F = U	**O** = L	**X** = C
G = T	**P** = K	**Y** = B
H = S	**Q** = J	**Z** = A
I = R	**R** = I	

Sea Creatures
1. WRYYLSVFU
2. JUNYR
3. CBECBVFR
4. QBYCUVA
5. BPGBCHF
6. FRNUBEFR
7. FGNESVFU
8. FDHVQ

Vegetables
1. XZFORUOLDVI
2. YVVG
3. YVZM
4. XZIILG
5. OVGGFXV
6. YILXXLOR
7. XLIM
8. XVOVIB

Answer on page 35.

YO-YO U.

These freshmen at Yo-Yo University were studying for their first big test when this happened. Can you tell which yo-yo belongs to each student?

Answer on page 35.

Illustrated by Barbara Gray

SOUR NOTES

How many things can you find wrong in this picture?

WORLD OF COLOR

These words are hidden in the letters you see
below. Look up, down, sideways, backwards, and
diagonally. Some letters are used more than once.
When you find a word, circle it. After you finish,
put the leftover letters in the blank spaces to spell
a colorful message.

AQUA
PINK
BEIGE
PURPLE
BLACK
RED
BLUE
SHADE
BROWN
SHINY

COLOR WHEEL
SILVER
DARK
SPECTRUM
DULL
TAN
GOLD
TINT
GREEN
TRANSPARENT

GRAY
TURQUOISE
HUE
VIBRANT
ORCHID
VIOLET
LIGHT
WHITE
ORANGE
YELLOW

```
E Y E L L O W A L T R S
T R A N S P A R E N T P
I A E I N A B E I T R E
H N B D G Q H I T E V C
W E L P R U P W B V L T
W T O I E A Y R E I I R
V H R N E O A O L S S U
I G C K N R W K G D D M
O I H E G N A L O E L D
L L I F C B L C K O O U
E O D L S H A E L R G L
T U R Q U O I D E R I L
V I B R A N T S H N Y
```

Message:

_ _ _ _ _ _ _ _ _ _ _ _ _ _

Answer on page 35.

Illustrated by Doug Taylor

PICKY'S PEACHES

Picky keeps his peach trees in perfect shape. In every row of trees, down, across, and diagonally, there are thirty peaches. Picky can tell how many peaches grow on each tree by the number of peaches on the corner trees. Can you?

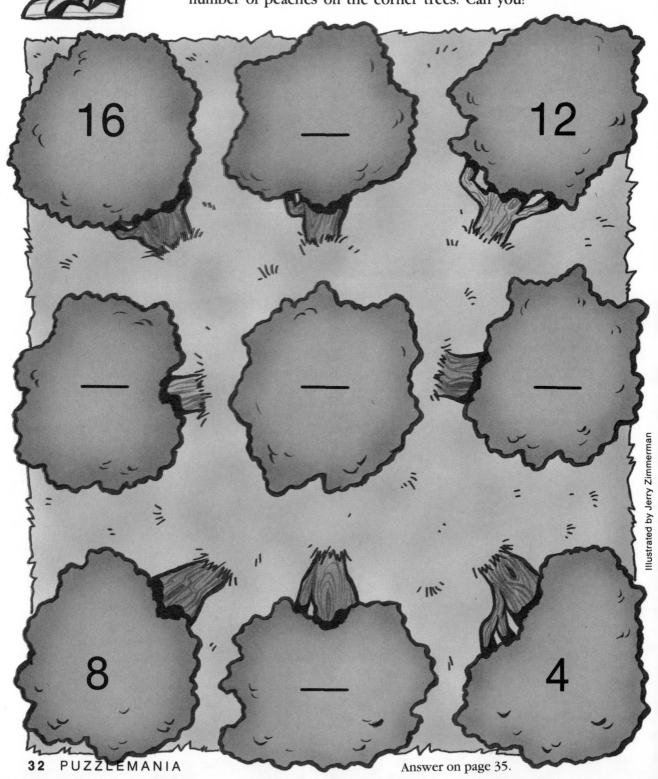

Illustrated by Jerry Zimmerman

Answer on page 35.